T0193982

Who'da Thunk It?

Elmer Hembree

WESTBOW
PRESS®
A DIVISION OF THOMAS NELSON
& ZONDERVAN

Scripture quotations are taken from the Holy Bible, New Living
Translation, copyright ©1996, 2004, 2007, 2013, 2015 by Tyndale
House Foundation. Used by permission of Tyndale House
Publishers, Inc., Carol Stream, Illinois 60188. All rights reserved.

WestBow Press books may be ordered through
booksellers or by contacting:

WestBow Press
A Division of Thomas Nelson & Zondervan
1663 Liberty Drive
Bloomington, IN 47403
www.westbowpress.com
1 (866) 928-1240

ISBN: 978-1-9736-2276-5 (sc)
ISBN: 978-1-9736-2275-8 (e)

Library of Congress Control Number: 2018903184

Print information available on the last page.

WestBow Press rev. date: 03/14/2018

To Josephine Dodson, a wonderful friend who was a devoted Christian for many years. She was a blessing to me and many other friends prior to her passing.

She went to be with Jesus, whom she loved and served with all of her heart. She was a person who displayed Christ in her life, even when she was suffering so much. She kept her eyes fixed on her Savior and looked for every opportunity to share God's love with as many people as she could.

I had the honor and privilege to serve her communion a few days before she went to heaven, and after I left her, I felt God spoke to me to dedicate this book to her.

Acknowledgments

A special thanks to Tiffany Crenshaw for her design of the cover of this book.

To Lamar Dodson for all the work he did in proofreading this book.

To my son Radford, who gave me the title for the book.

To my daughter, Rebecca, and son Robert, who encouraged me to complete this book.

To my wife, Janet, who was beside me each and every day, encouraging and helping me to stay on track while writing this book.

Preface

It is very amazing what you find when you read God's Word and how the Word of God grips your heart to the point you want to read as much as you can. On several occasions, I have been up the entire night, reading his Word.

I have read the entire Bible many times in my eighty-five years of life but had not taken the time to absorb and study as I should have done. Every time I start to read, I pray and ask God to reveal to me what he wants me to understand. In every instance, he gives me something I have to think about for a long time.

Years ago, my mother told me to watch what I said because "a little bird might tell someone what you said." I asked her where she heard that, and she told me she had read it in the Bible.

Not believing her, I asked where it was in the Bible. Her answer to me was, "You go find it." Well,

I did just that, and I found many other sayings that I have written and commented on in this book.

All scriptures listed throughout this book are taken from the New Living Translation (NLT).

1

Old Wives' Tales

When I was a small child, my mother used to tell me things I didn't understand and then say they were "old wives' tales."

Many years ago, an English novel explained that an old wives' tale was a type of urban legend similar to a proverb, which generally was passed down by old wives to a younger generation.

Such tales usually consisted of superstition, folklore, or unverified claims with exaggerated and/or untrue details.

Today, old wives' tales are still common among children on school playgrounds. Old wives' tales often concern pregnancy, puberty, and nutrition. It should be noted that this use of the word *wives* simply means women, rather than married women.

This usage stems from the Old English *wife (woman)* and is akin to the German *Weile,* also meaning woman. This sense of the word is still used in modern English in constructions such as *midwife* and *fishwife* (wife of a fisherman).

Almost all wives' tales are false and are used to discourage unwanted behavior, usually in children. Grandparents might have known of all kinds of teas and poultices, for example, that claimed to heal cuts and beestings, lower fevers, and more. Hence, the old wives' tales have been validated as being effective at what they claim to do, whereas in the past they were pretty much ridiculed by the medical community.

Now, that doesn't mean they rival modern medicine and that your doctor's advice should be ignored. But sometimes natural, alternative treatments can be used for certain maladies with good results and much less risk of side effects.

Here are some things that have been handed down over the years:

1. Always hang a horseshoe over your door with the ends up for good luck. If the ends point down, the luck will pour out.
2. You can measure the distance of a storm from the flash of the lightning to the sound of thunder.
3. When the wind blows the leaves on the trees upside down, there will be a heavy rain.

4. If the deer are out early grazing, there is a big storm coming.
5. Winter thunder means snow within ten days.
6. If you drop a fork on the floor, you'll get money.

Now let us look at 1 Timothy 4:7, which says, "Do not waste time arguing over godless ideas and old wives' tales. Instead, train yourself to be godly."

Paul was talking to the false teachers and affirmed that everything God created is good. Genesis 1 tells us that we should ask for God's blessing on his created gifts that give us pleasure and thank him for them. This doesn't mean that we should abuse what God has made.

We should always thank God for the love he shows us. I'm not sure if I could go one day without God's love. Dependence on his love will always guide us into new biblical truths.

We all are given gifts from the Lord and should exercise these gifts on a daily basis. As we walk with the Lord, by faith, he always will strengthen and guide us into the truth.

Paul was trying to reach these young widows by challenging them to trust in God, rather than trusting the false teachers.

This is why we work hard and continue to struggle, for our hope is in the living God, who is the Savior of all the people and particularly of all believers. (1 Timothy 4:10)

Don't let them waste their time in endless discussion of myths and spiritual pedigrees. These things only lead to meaningless speculations, which don't help people live a life of faith in God. (1 Timothy 1:4)

Don't let anyone capture you with empty philosophies and high-sounding nonsense that come from human thinking and from spiritual powers of this world, rather than from Christ. (Colossians 2:8)

There appear to be many new teachings that are contrary to what we have been taught in the past. The result of teachings should cause us to study God's Word each and every day.

A lot of these philosophies depend on human wisdom and the spiritual customs of this world, rather on Christ.

Paul was attempting to open the eyes of individuals with whom he had been in contact on one of his journeys.

When my mother didn't tell me where in the Bible the old wives' tales were mentioned, she caused me to search the scriptures and find it myself. And I did just that! And that led to me finding many other sayings I have placed in this book. They are very interesting, to say the least.

What we as Christians need to do in this present time is to read God's Word and share with others to help them grow in faith.

2

A Nudge of the Foot or a Wiggle of the Fingers

What are worthless and wicked people like? They are constant liars, signaling their deceit with a wink of the eye, a nudge of the foot, or wiggle of fingers.

—Proverbs 6:12–13

Let me give you an illustration about a flock of sheep that broke into three groups.

The first group of sheep decided to look to the shepherd and follow him wherever he led. John 10:27 says, "My sheep listen to my voice; I know them and they follow me."

The second group wanted nothing to do with the shepherd. They wanted to run their lives their own way and deliberately decided to walk away from him. These were the pagans and atheists of society. They didn't want to hear Jesus's voice. They didn't want to follow.

The third group decided that they liked the shepherd. They wanted to hang out with him, but they didn't want to get too close to him. They still wanted to keep their options open. They wanted to look for their own grass once in a while. They wanted to nibble at a little of this and a little of that.

The problem with this third group of sheep is that they're the ones who end up getting lost. They're just close enough to the shepherd to feel secure—and just far enough away to not hear his voice.

Sometimes they wander off into their own little world and end up getting hurt and making bad decisions. These bad decisions cause them pain and heartache.

That's the way it is with those who try to live for the Lord and the pleasures of this world at the same time. Trying to walk two roads can only lead to blisters in the end.

Proverbs 12:15 says, "Fools think their own way is right, but the wise listen to others."

God created us, knows us, and loves us. It only makes sense to listen to his instructions and do what he says. The Bible is his unfailing word to us. It is like an owner's manual for the car. If you obey God's instructions, you will "run right" and find his kind of power to live. If you ignore them, you will have breakdowns, accidents, and failures.

Blameless living safeguards your life. Each choice for good sets into motion other opportunities for good. Evil choices follow the same pattern but in the opposite direction.

Each decision you make to obey God's Word will bring a greater sense of order in your life, while each decision to disobey will bring confusion and destruction.

The right choices you make reflect your integrity. Obedience brings the greatest safeguard and security. When we don't listen to the Good Shepherd or follow him closely, we will be without the protection of that Shepherd and open to attacks of Satan and this world.

Follow the voice of the Shepherd, and he will never let you down.

3

Escaped Death by the Skin of My Teeth

I have been reduced to skin and bones and have escaped death by the skin of my teeth.

—Job 19:20

Job felt that God was treating him as an enemy when, in fact, God was his friend and thought highly of him.

Job 1:8 says, "Then the Lord asked Satan, 'Have you noticed my servant Job? He is the finest man in all the earth. He is blameless—a man of complete integrity. He fears God and stays away from evil.'"

Job had a very hard life. He had boils, bereavements, bankruptcy, and a foolish wife, who told him to curse God and die, and he wished he was dead. Job was wasting away and cried out, "I have escaped death by the skin of my teeth."

This is a very narrow escape, you say, for Job's body and soul, but there are thousands of men who make just as narrow an escape for their souls. There was a time when the partition between them and ruin was no thicker than a tooth's enamel, but as Job finally escaped, so have they.

Job did not hide his overwhelming grief. He had not lost his faith in God; instead, his emotions showed that he was human and that he loved his family.

Satan was allowed to test Job, but he lost the first round. Job was suffering very much, and his so-called friends came to comfort him, but they did nothing to help. Let us look at what some of his friends said to him.

Eliphaz the Temanite—Job 4–5, 15:22. "He sat in silence with Job for seven days. He said Job was suffering because he has sinned. He said for Job to go to God and present his case." Job's response was this: "Stop assuming my guilt." God rebuked Job's friends.

Bildad the Shuhite—Job 8:18. "He sat in silence with Job for seven days. He said Job wouldn't admit he sinned, so he's still suffering. His advice to Job, "How long will you go on like this?" Job's response: "I will say to God, tell me the charges you are bringing against me." God rebuked Job's friends."

Zohar the Naamothite—Job 11:20. "He sat in silence with Job for seven days. He said Job's sin deserves even more suffering than he's experienced. He told Job to, "Get rid of his sins." Job said, "I will be proved innocent. "God rebukes Job's friends."

Elihu the Busite—Job 32:37. "He sat in silence with Job for seven days. He said to Job, "God is using suffering to mold and train him." His advice to Job was, "Keep silent and I will teach you wisdom." Job gave no response to this; God rebuked Job's friends."

Job 38:41. "God confronted Job with the need to be content even though he didn't know why he was suffering. God did not explain the reason for the pain. His advice to Job: "Do you still want to argue with the almighty?" Job's response to God was, "I was talking about things I did not understand."

Job was very confident that God's justice would triumph over all of what Satan had been doing to him. Instead of becoming angry with God, Job continued to trust that God would be with him through all of his troubles.

Sometimes even though it is difficult to see, God is in control. We must commit ourselves to him so we will not resent his timing.

The next time you face trials and dilemmas, see them as opportunities to turn to God for strength. You will find a God who only desires to show his love and compassion for you. Make God your foundation. You can never be separated from his love.

"So the Lord blessed Job in the second half of his life even more than in the beginning" (Job 42:12).

4

Icy Breath of God

God's breath sends the ice, freezing
wide expanses of water.

—Job 37:10

The changes in the weather are the subject of a great deal of our thoughts and common talk, but how seldom do we think and speak of these things with regard to God?

God is the director of the weather, and we must notice the glory of God not only in the thunder and lightning but in the more common and less awful changes of the weather, such as snow and rain.

We don't have the freezing rain and snow here in southern Texas that they have up around Dallas, Fort Worth, Amarillo, or in the northern states and Alaska.

Many times people will murmur about the weather, knowing that God alone is the one who controls it. The changes and extremes of the weather, wet or dry, hot or cold, are the subject of a great deal of our common talk and observation.

We must take notice of the glory of God, not only in the thunder and lightning, but in the more common revolutions of the weather. Just as God has a powerful, freezing north wind, he has a thawing, composing south wind. The Spirit is compared to both because God convinces and comforts.

"Listen carefully to the thunder of God's voice as it rolls from his mouth" (Job 37:2).

Do you remember how you felt when you were very young and your birthday approached? You were excited and eager. You knew you certainly would receive gifts and other special treats, but some things would be a surprise. Birthdays combine assurance and anticipation, and so does faith. Faith is confidence based on past experience that God's new and fresh surprises will surely be ours.

The beginning point of faith is believing in God's character. He is who he says he is. The end point is believing in God's promises. He will do what he says. When we believe that God will fulfill his promises materializing yet, we demonstrate true faith.

Then Jesus told him, "You believe because you have seen me. Blessed are those who believe without seeing me." This was what Jesus told Thomas when he saw Jesus the second time after Jesus' resurrection. (John 20:29)

Have you ever wished you could actually see Jesus, touch him, and hear his words? Are there times you want to sit down with him and get his advice?

Jesus is the only person we can lean on and be safe. Our foundation is secured only with Jesus Christ.

Trust in him.

5

Shortest Short Story

There was a small town with only a
few people, and a great king came
with his army and besieged it. A poor
wise man knew how to save the town,
and so it was rescued. But afterward
no one thought to thank him.

—Ecclesiastes 9:14–15

The passage above is the shortest short story I
know in the Bible.

Sometimes we fail to thank the person who
has helped us through a problem, as the scripture
indicated.

Most of society looks at wealth, success, and
accomplishments and places them above wisdom.
Sometimes the poor individuals have more wisdom

that those who claim to have all knowledge of the world.

We can learn from this scripture about the poor wise man, and it will help us to do God's will in many ways.

Let us look at the meanings of the word *wisdom*.

1. Good sense: It is the ability to make sensible decisions and judgments, based on personal knowledge and experience.
2. Wise decision: It is good sense shown in a way of thinking, judgment, or action.
3. Accumulated learning: It is the accumulated knowledge of life or of a sphere of activity that has been gained through experience.

Sometimes we seek wisdom from the wrong things or people.

> The woman was convinced. She saw that the tree was beautiful and its fruit looked delicious, and she wanted the wisdom it would give her. So she took some of the fruit and ate it. Then she gave some to her husband, who was with her, and he ate it, too. (Genesis 3:6)

Satan tried to make Eve think that sin was good, pleasant, and desirable. Knowledge of both good and evil seemed harmless to her. People usually choose wrong things because they have become convinced that those things are good, at least for themselves.

Our sins do not always appear ugly to us, and pleasant sins are hard to avoid. So prepare yourself for the attractive temptations that may come your way. Use God's Word and God's people to help you stand against it.

Notice what Eve did:

1. She looked.
2. She took.
3. She ate.
4. She gave.

The battle is often lost at the first look. Temptation often begins by simply seeing something you want.

Look at the last sentence of Ecclesiastes 9:16—"But afterword no one thought to thank him." The wise man saved the city, but no one thanked him for the good he did for them.

"Don't worry about anything, instead, pray about everything" (Philippians 4:6). Imagine never worrying about anything! It seems like an impossibility. We all have worries on the job, in our lives, in our homes, here in this place, and about our children and grandchildren.

But Paul's advice is to turn our worries into prayers. Do you want to worry less? Then pray more.

> Therefore, we never stop thanking God that when we received his message from us, you didn't think of our words as mere human ideas. You accepted what we said as the very word of God—which, of course, it is. And this word continues to work in you who believe. (1 Thessalonians 2:13)

When God answers prayers, works miracles, and guides you through everyday life, stop and give him praise for what he has done for you.

In all things, give thanks to God.

6

Closing the Eyes of the Corpse

I will go with you down to Egypt,
and I will bring you back again. You
will die in Egypt but Joseph will be
with you to close your eyes.

—Genesis 46:4

Jacob arriving at Beersheba is encouraged by
a revelation from God. Beersheba may be
regarded as the fourth scene of Abraham's abode
in the Land of Promise. From the Lord's words to
Abraham and the way in which Joseph's dreams
were realized in the events of providence, Jacob
had gathered that his family was to descend into

Egypt. He felt that by taking this step, he was obeying the will of heaven.

"I am God, the God of your father, the voice said. Don't be afraid to go down to Egypt, for there I will make your family into a great nation" (Genesis 46:3). He approached God in sacrifice at an old abode of Abraham and Isaac before he crossed the border into Egypt. On this solemn occasion, God appeared to him in the visions of the night. He designated himself as *El-Shaddai*, the mighty and the God of his father.

When God told him, "Do not be afraid to go down to Egypt," this implies that it was the will of God that he should go down to Egypt and that he would be protected there—"a great nation."

Jacob now had a large family, of whom no longer was selected, but all were included in the chosen seed. He had received the special blessing and injunction to be fruitful and multiply.

"May God Almighty bless you and give you many children. And may your descendants multiply and become many nations!" (Genesis 28:3). The chosen family was to be the beginning of the chosen nation. "I will go with you down to Egypt." The "I" here is emphatic, as it is in the assurance that God will bring him up in the fullness of time for Egypt.

If Israel, in the process of growth from family to a nation, had remained among the Canaanites, he would have been amalgamated with the nation by intermarriage and would have conformed to its vices. By his removal to Egypt, he was kept apart from the demoralizing influence of a nation whose iniquity became as great to demand a judicial extirpation shepherd as he was, is an abomination to Egypt.

By his location in the comparatively high land of Goshen and by the reduction of his race to a body of serfs, the nation would not condescend to intermingle. His long-lost son would be parent to perform the last offices to him when deceased. "You will die in Egypt, but Joseph will be with you to close your eyes."

When new situations or surroundings frighten you, recognize that experiencing fear is normal. To be paralyzed by fear, however, is an indication that you question God's ability to take care of you.

Jacob never returned to Canaan, but God promised that his descendants would return. Jacob would die in Egypt, with Joseph at his side. God's promise to Jacob was that he would never know the pain of being lonely again.

It is not likely that Jacob would have attempted to go down to Egypt if he had not received these assurances from God, and it is very likely that he offered his sacrifice merely to obtain this information.

The closing of the eyes was a custom among the Greeks and Romans. In my younger days, people used to put pennies on the eyelids of the deceased to keep them closed. Now the eyelids are glued closed.

Remember this: "Those that go where God sends them shall certainly have God with them."

Jacob died in Egypt, yet this promise was fulfilled in bringing his body to be buried in Canaan. Whatever low and dark valley we are called into, we may be confident that if God will go down with us, he surely will bring us up again.

That is a promise that Joseph lived by as long as he lived—that he should be with him in his death and close his eyes with all possible tenderness.

Listen to God's voice!

7

Leaning on a
Spider's Web

Their confidence hangs by a thread;
they are leaning on a spiders web.

—Job 8:14

Confidence is the faith or belief that one will act in a right and proper, effective way; it's a feeling of consciousness of one's powers, a quality or state of being certain.

> Don't put your confidence in powerful
> people; there is no help for you there.
> (Psalm 146:3)

> But joyful are those who have the
> God of Israel as their helper, whose
> hope is in the Lord their God. (Psalm
> 146:5)

When the world seems out of control, we must remind ourselves that God owns the cities and knows the future of every nation. When God is in control of our lives, his help will ensure we gain the victory.

> This is what the Sovereign Lord,
> the Holy one of Israel, says only in
> returning to me and resting in me
> will you be saved. In quietness and
> confidence is your strength. But you
> would have none of it. (Isaiah 30:15)

We all know how flimsy a spider's web is. The spider spins the web, encloses itself in it, and dwells securely—or so it thinks. The spider's web is a very nice and a curious piece of workmanship.

The same is like the outward work of righteous done by hypocrites appear to be seen of men, yet are very thin and will bear no weight at all.

We make a fine appearance but have no substance, and things are done without the strength of Christ or the Glory of God. These all fall short of bearing the weight of the salvation of the soul.

The spider's web is spun out of its bowels, and so is the work of such persons who are wholly of themselves, without the grace of God and the spirit of Christ. These webs are not fit for garments, are too thin to cover naked souls, and are insufficient to shelter from the wrath of God.

These webs cannot bear the broom of justice. One stroke can sweep them away, even when they feel themselves safe in their webs.

We may find ourselves in the issue of mistaken. There is none but Christ and his righteous.

> Then the Lord answered from the whirlwind: "Who is this that questions my wisdom with such ignorant words?" (Job 38:1–2)

> You asked, "Who is this that questions my wisdom with such ignorance?" It is I—and I was talking bout things I knew nothing about, things far too wonderful for me. (Job 41:2)

Surprisingly, he didn't answer any of Job's questions. Job's questions were not at the heart of the issue. Instead, God used Job's ignorance of the earth's natural order to reveal his ignorance of God's moral order. If Job did not understand the working of God's physical creation, how could he possibly understand the working of God's physical creation? How could he possibly understand God's mind and character?

Job admitted that he was the one who had been foolish. We also must admit to God that we don't ever have enough faith to trust him.

God reveals his great power in nature. We can trust God to give us both the peace and strength to weather the storms of life.

Lean on Jesus Christ, and you will always be safe.

8

Fish-Scale Blindness

Instantly something like scales fell from Saul's eyes and he regained his sight.

—Acts 9:18

The beginning of Acts 9 records the conversion of Saul of Tarsus, and we discover that something was going on in Saul's conscience before the Lord met him on the Damascus road.

When we look at the scripture, we cannot fail to be convinced that Paul's conversion was sudden. The actual moment when the Lord took hold of him and when he was brought as a humble penitent to the feet of the Savior took place in a moment of time.

At that moment, he was an enemy, and in the next moment, he was an inquirer with a broken and contrite heart and a longing to do the will of the risen Lord. In this sense, every conversion is sudden.

When we enter into an experience of the salvation that is in Christ Jesus, we do not always know the exact moment of our conversion.

Our conversion takes place suddenly. We are born again, and our lives are changed.

God's plan for Paul was that he should become the apostle to the Gentiles. God has a plan for your life and mine. It should be our chief concern to discover and to do the will of God.

Paul's conversion had an immediate relation to the conversion of many individuals in the future. What a challenging thought, for it is also true of every Christian! When God saved us, it was with a view to the salvation of others in our families, those with whom we work, others whose lives we touch, and those to whom we would minister the Word of God.

We marvel at the fact that this persecutor, enemy, and leader of the anti-Christian group was suddenly and completely changed from his old life into a humble, inquiring, penitent follower and an obedient servant of the Lord.

He was completely transformed from his old way of life to be a completely different person. When a person is truly converted, certain things always happen. There are certain marks that show the reality of their conversions.

The following was true of Saul of Tarsus:

- He met with the Lord and heard his voice.
- He was filled with a longing to obey the Lord and to do his will,
- He began to pray.
- He was baptized.
- He united in fellowship with God's people.
- He began to testify powerfully.
- He grew in grace.

"Something like scales fell from Saul's eyes and he regained his sight."

9

Long Hike, No Blisters

> For all these forty years your clothes didn't wear out and your feet didn't blister or smell.
>
> —Deuteronomy 8:4

Sometimes in life we take God's protection for granted, wondering if God does care for us.

"For forty years I led you through the wilderness, yet your clothes and sandals did not wear out" (Deuteronomy 29:5). Think about this for a minute. They wandered around in the wilderness for forty years, and their clothes and sandals did not wear out. When I was in school, I remember wearing out a pair of shoes during the school year. If I didn't wear them out, I grew so much that they no longer fit. When that happened, I was told I had to wear my brother's shoes, which he had outgrown also. I had to wear his hand-me-down clothes also, and that upset me something awful. My dad and mother would cry when I was upset about wearing these clothes. They were not financially able to buy any more clothes or shoes. I remember that during World War II, shoes were rationed.

The children of Israel were not aware of how God took care of them throughout their journey. They wandered and grumbled about God's not providing things for them.

> Remember how the Lord your God led you through the wilderness for these forty years, humbling you and testing you to prove your character, and to find out whether or not you would obey his commands. Yes, he humbled you by letting you go hungry and then feeding you with manna, a food previously unknown to you or your ancestors. He did it to teach you that people did not live by bread alone, rather, we live by every word that comes from the mouth of the Lord. (Deuteronomy 8:2–3)

Jesus quoted Deuteronomy 8:3 when the devil tempted him to turn stones into bread. "If you are the Son of God tell these stones to become loaves of bread."

I was in Korea during the conflict there, and the first time I went to the chow hall to eat breakfast, I was handed a box of what they called C-rations. In this small box was all the food for the entire day. I complained, along with other individuals, about how distasteful these things were. There was not enough food for the entire day, and we stayed hungry until we learned to not eat all of it at once.

Sometimes we think life is based on satisfying our appetites. If we earn enough money to dress, eat, and play in high style, we think we are living "the good life." If things do not satisfy us, however, we grumble, and this leaves us empty and dissatisfied.

Real life, according to Moses, "comes from total commitment to God and living by every word the comes from Him."

The following tells us how we can live by his Word:

1. Agree that God alone can truly satisfy you.
2. Pray for God's presence, wisdom, and direction as you read.

3. Savor the relationship you have with him through Christ.
4. Practice what he teaches you.

God was always with the Israelites, even though they grumbled and complained daily about everything. In spite of their repeated complaining, stubbornness, and self-pride, God never failed them. He guided them in their journey through the wilderness.

> For the Lord your God has blessed you in everything you have done, He has watched your every step through the great wilderness. During these forty years, the Lord your God has been with you, and you have lacked nothing. (Deuteronomy 2:7)

God can and will take care of us, even in today's society.

9

Tax-Paying Fish

However, we don't want to offend
them, so go down to the lake and
throw in a line. Open the mouth of
the first fish you catch, and you will
find a large silver coin. Take it and
pay the tax for both of us.

—Matthew 17:27

I can see Peter just shaking his head. All they
wanted was money. Couldn't they see the bigger
picture? There was more at stake than just money.
They had just arrived back in town, and before they
could even get settled, the Roman government was
there with its hand out.

The people around Peter wanted to know if
Jesus had paid his share of the temple tax for the

year. I don't really know what Peter knew, so he did what most of us would do: he bluffed.

You see, the tax had been established 1,400 years earlier, when the people of Israel were still in the wilderness. And its purpose was to provide for the upkeep and maintenance of the tabernacle, which was like a portable temple, where the high priest performed the required sacrifices.

And while the average Israelites probably never thought about it, there would have been considerable expense in maintaining the tabernacle. The Israelites had no earning power when they were wandering around in the desert in search of the Promised Land.

What the people did have was the accumulated savings that they had brought with them. And so a tax was levied on them, one-half of a shekel. This wasn't a portly sum in that day, but if they were going to maintain a place of worship, then sacrifice was needed, and they would have to give beyond what was easy. By the time of Jesus, however, everyone was happily paying taxes. As a matter of fact, some nationalists and zealots refused to pay the taxes as long as Jerusalem was occupied by a foreign army. In this case, it was the Roman army.

The real question was whether those who questioned Peter were really interested in getting the temple tax or if they were setting up Jesus. So when they asked Peter, "Doesn't your teacher pay the temple tax?", Peter immediately said, "Yes, he does."

Then he went to ask Jesus if he had paid his tax. Before Peter even could open his mouth, Jesus began to teach him.

> "What do you think Peter? Do kings tax their own people or the people they have conquered?" "They tax the people they have conquered, Peter replied. Well then, Jesus said the citizens are free." (Matthew 17:25–26)

Peter knew how to catch fish, but Jesus would also teach him how to bring people into his kingdom. I also wonder whether Jesus's eyes twinkled a little when he told Peter to cast a hook without bait into the sea. Peter had to have faith to go fishing after Jesus instructed him to do so and without any bait on the hook.

He was testing Peter's faith when he told him to go fish, which was Peter's area of expertise. It is very often our strengths, rather than our weaknesses, that keep us from obeying and depending on the Lord.

Even those who have never fished would know that fish don't swim around with coins in their mouths. In verse 17, Jesus got to the heart of the matter when he said, "We don't want to offend them."

Jesus was not obligated to pay a tax to a temple that belonged to his Father. Jesus, however, paid it anyway. By doing so with the money delivered by a fish, Jesus avoided one reason someone might have used to reject him. By paying the temple tax, the tax collectors would have the opportunity to accept him as their personal Savior.

When Jesus allowed himself to be crucified by evil people, he suffered on our behalf to pay the price for our sins.

> Even though I am a free man with no master, I have become a slave to all people to bring many to Christ. (1 Corinthians 9:19)

Jesus is the way, the truth, and the life! And we always must have faith in him, even though it may seem a little bit odd to us.

10

Sold for Nothing

For this is what the Lord says; when I sold you into exile, I received my payment. Now I can redeem you without having to pay for you.

—Isaiah 52:3

"You shall be redeemed without money." The truth is more fully stated in Isaiah 55:1, which states, "Is anyone thirsty? Come and drink even if you have no money; come, take your choice of wine or milk—it's all free!" Food costs money, lasts only a short time, and meets only physical needs. God offers us free nourishment that feeds our souls.

How do we get it?

- Isaiah 55:1 says, "Come and drink."
- Isaiah 55: 2 says, "Listen."
- Isaiah 55:6 says, "Seek and call on God."

The story of a "pearl of great price" illustrates what returning to a regenerate Jerusalem was like for the captives. If they put their wealth together, what kind of a relationship would they have, helping to restore Jerusalem?

> For you know that God paid a ransom to save you from the empty life you inherited from your ancestors. And the ransom he paid was not mere gold or silver. It was the precious blood of Christ, the sinless, spotless Lamb of God. (1 Peter 1:18–19)

The value of this redemption could not be measured by human wealth; that would be so great a price that we could not pay. Our redemption is priceless and cannot be bought for any price.

I remember, years ago, I was at my sister's father-in-law's home, looking at the coon dogs he raised and sold. A man came up and asked if he could buy a particular dog. Allen said he wouldn't sell his best dog for any price. This man said, "I have a thousand dollars in my pocket right now, and I will give you that and go get two thousand more if you will sell me that dog."

Allen looked at him and said, "You don't have enough money in your bank account to pay for that dog. He is not for sale at any price."

God's redemption is also priceless. He does not want to sell. It can be received only as a gift from Christ.

> And this is the way to have eternal life—to know you, the only true God, and Jesus Christ, the one you sent to earth. (John 17:3)

Jesus Christ has already paid the price for all who seek him.

11

Silent Witness

In the same way, you wives must accept the authority of your husbands. Then, even if some refuse to obey the Good News, your godly lives will speak to them without any words. They will be won over by observing your pure and reverent lives.

—1 Peter 3:1–2

The words here are "speak to them without any words." When we live a holy life before our friends, neighbors, and coworkers, we will see that we are different, and without speaking a word to them, they will see Christ in us.

How does it feel to know you are special and loved? How does it feel to be promoted or to be set apart for special favor? When someone talks about you to another person, saying how wonderful you have been to him or her, how does that make you feel?

In this passage and in this book, Peter seeks to encourage Christians who are being mistreated and persecuted for their faith. They were scattered among five Roman provinces in what became modern-day Turkey, probably seeking to hide in safety from Nero, who was burning Christians at the stake and confiscating their lands.

Peter sought encourage them by sharing with them how special they were to God and that their "godly lives will speak to them without any words."

When I was a small child, all my dad had to do was look at me with his stern face, not saying a word, and I would know what he was talking about. There is an old saying: Actions speak louder than words.

Marriage is one of the most important human relationships. No wonder Peter offered a few sentences to help his readers with this sometimes difficult institution.

But Peter's thoughts weren't confined to marriage. He was very concerned about all kinds of relationships in society—with government, with masters and slaves, and with marriages. He knew that if Christians were perceived as societal rebels and radicals, their message wouldn't be heard, and the Christian faith wouldn't grow.

When he said "in the same way," he was referring to his comments about submission to governments and to masters. The key here is voluntary submission. Peter wasn't demanding obedience, although obedience is involved with submission. He was asking for an attitude toward one's husband of voluntary submission, whether or not he was a Christian.

Our behavior must convince individuals, not our words. You can't talk your husband or anyone else into the kingdom. You must be willing to live out your Christianity to everyone. They must observe it in action; then your words may not be superfluous. Think of your behavior as an investment into others' lives by the way you live yours.

I would like you to think about four words:

1. Reverence
2. Purity
3. Gentleness
4. Quiet

How do you come by this kind of character? We choose to regularly yield to the Spirit of God and let that Spirit reign in our lives. From the "abiding presence of the Holy Spirit come his fruits— love, joy, peace, patience, kindness, goodness, faithfulness, gentleness, and self-control.

> But the Holy Spirit produces this kind of fruit in our lives; Love, joy, peace, patience, kindness, goodness, faithfulness, gentleness, and self-control. There is no law against these things. (Galatians 5:22–23)

God looks on your heart and smiles in enjoyment of your character, which he values so highly.

We need to pray daily for forgiveness for our selfishness and attempts to dominate. We need to work to exhibit the fruit of God's Spirit both inside of us and in the way we relate to others.

As I said, actions speak louder than words.

12

Actions Speak Louder than Words

I have heard this statement many times during my lifetime, often from my father and mother. It's amazing what you find in the Bible when you study God's Word.

Remember when you were in English class and learned about oral, written, and nonverbal skills? Oral communication is the ability to explain and present your ideas in clear English. Written communication is the ability to write effectively on a range of topics. Nonverbal communication is the ability to enhance the expression of ideas through the use of body language.

> If someone has enough money to live well and sees a brother or sister in need but shows no compassion—how

> can God's love be in that person? Dear children, let's not merely say we love each other; let us show the truth by our actions. Our actions will show that we belong to the truth, so we will be confident when we stand before God. (1 John 3:17–19)

These verses give a wonderful example of how we can live our lives in our daily walk with Jesus Christ.

I was in a drugstore several months ago, waiting in line to pick up a prescription, when I noticed that an elderly lady, two people ahead of me in line, was having problems with coming up with enough money to purchase her medicine. I overheard her tell the sales person that she only had enough money to pay for two of the three items she came to pick up.

Without saying anything to this lady, the man in front of me handed the sales person the money to purchase the third bottle for her. The lady turned around with tears in her eyes and thanked him for this wonderful thing he had done for her.

Sometime later, I walked into my doctor's office for an appointment. As I waited to sign in to let them know I was there, an aged, frail lady told the attendant at the desk that she was there for her appointment. The attendant looked at the computer for the lady's name, but it wasn't listed for that date; her appointment was for the next day. This lady was very upset at herself for not remembering the right date because she had to catch a bus to get there. She asked if the doctor could see her anyway.

The attendant checked with the doctor, who agreed to see her. The attendant then informed the lady that there was a twenty-five-dollar co-pay. The lady said she didn't understand about the co-pay; she didn't have enough money to pay it and still have bus money to return home.

I then remembered the situation with the lady at the drugstore, and I felt so sorry for this lady that I pulled out twenty-five dollars and handed it to the attendant so the lady could see the doctor. The elderly lady turned around, smiled at me, and said, "What a nice young man you are to help me."

When she went in to see the doctor, the attendant handed the twenty-five dollars back to me, saying the doctor said he would waive the co-pay.

Both of these stories actually happened and are good examples of actions speaking louder than words.

Jesus said,

> For I was hungry, and you fed me. I was thirsty and you gave me drink.

> I was a stranger and you invited me into your home. I was naked and you gave me clothing. I was sick and you cared for me. I was in prison, and you visited me. (Matthew 25:35–36)

Acts of mercy could happen each and every day. You might see this as you travel to and from work. A lady has a flat tire, and individuals stop to assist her. Or a person who runs out of gas is walking down the highway or street, carrying a gas can, and someone stops to pick him up and take him to a gas station and then back to his car.

Without God, life's problems have no lasting solutions!

Our actions speak louder than words.

13

Chasing the Wind

But as I looked at everything I had
worked so hard to accomplish, it
was all so meaningless-like chasing
the wind. There was nothing really
worthwhile anywhere.

—Ecclesiastes 2:11

I don't know if my math teachers ever read the
Bible, but if they did, they would have been
pleased to read Ecclesiastes. It is a book that shows
us the math for the rest of the Bible.

My teacher always wanted us to show how we
arrived at the answers to the questions she gave to
us. On occasion, I couldn't understand the proper
way to work the problem. When this occurred, I
would ask my friend what his answer was, and I

would write the answer on my paper. When the teacher graded my paper, she would lower my grade because I didn't show how I had arrived at the answer.

The Bible tells us that life apart from God lacks meaning; nothing apart from God is satisfying. Life is short, and there's no time to waste. In Ecclesiastes, we see how and why history's wisest fool arrived at these conclusions.

Solomon's answer is as timely as ever. We are blessed to live in the United States, as it is an experiment in "life, liberty, and the pursuit of happiness." As we see every day, this experiment is not going very well. Like Solomon, we live relatively lavish and luxurious lives in comparison to other parts of the world. Yet many of us are stressed and depressed over the economy, jobs, money, retirement, and many other areas.

We also spend much of our lives worrying that what we hate will destroy us. We live in fear that someone or something that we do not enjoy will overtake us and ruin our lives. We drive down the highway, wondering if someone is going to shoot at us. Or we park our car while we go shopping, and when we come out, our car is missing.

We must keep in mind that God has given us work to do. This is a gift from God, and we must trust him to help us in our daily lives. God has a plan for all of us, and it is our duty to follow that plan.

Because we are created in God's image, we have a spiritual thirst and eternal values, and nothing but the eternal God can truly satisfy us.

We must trust God now and do his work on earth, without chasing the wind.

14

You Have Collected All My Tears in Your Bottle

You keep track of all my sorrows. You have collected all my tears in your bottle. You have recorded each one in your book.

—Psalm 56:8

David's problem with Saul's trying to kill him was a daily battle for him. David's experiences, while far from his father's house and while in exile among those who hated him, became very lonely.

In the above verse, God says he keeps track of all the things that make us weep, and he records them in a book. He is like our parents; when we fall down and cry, God wipes away our tears with his gentle hand and gently places each tear in a bottle.

A man once told me that he was embarrassed to cry because it was not manly. After I read this verse to him, he was amazed that God would collect his tears and place them in a bottle. I reminded him about Jesus, who prayed in the garden and wept before his Father.

I asked myself this question: Why would God collect all my tears in a bottle? "Those who plant in tears will harvest with shouts of joy" (Psalm 126:5). I believe when we get to heaven, God will pour out those tears from the bottle and will turn those tears to joy.

So the next time you weep, just remember that your tears are being placed in a bottle. When you weep, you will know God is watching over you. He also will gently wrap his arms around you to protect you.

"But when I am afraid, I will put my trust in you" (Psalm 56:3). In the last sentence of verse 4, David said, "What can mere mortals do to me?"

> For God loved the world so much
> that he gave his one and only Son,
> so that everyone who believes in him
> will not perish but have eternal life.
> (John 3:16)

When it appears that we are on the run, it is time to remember God has called us and ordained us to do work for him. Satan does not want you to pay attention to what God wants you to do. What God has given you is yours. It is not the enemy's to control.

> My enemie will retreat when I call to
> you for help. This I know; God is on
> my side. (Psalm 56:9)

Jesus always cares for us and helps us through our troubled times.

> For you have rescued me from death;
> you have kept my feet from slipping.
> So now I can walk in your presence,
> O God, in your life-giving, light.
> (Psalm 56:13)

15

Wink at Their Treachery

O Lord my God, my holy One you who are eternal surely you do not plan to wipe us out? O Lord, our Rock, you have sent these Babylonians to correct us, to punish us for our many sins. But you are pure and cannot stand the sight of evil. Will you wink at their treachery? Should you be silent while the wicked swallow up people more righteous than they?

—Habakkuk 1:12–13

I was in a hospital room, visiting one of the members of the church who was dying; her two daughters were by her side. All day these daughters had been praying vigorously and passionately, but when I came into the hospital room, one of the daughters whispered to me, "I can't seem to get my prayers past the ceiling."

How many times have we stood before a silent God and wondered why our prayers were not answered? Why do our prayers go unanswered? Or do they?

On September 11, 2001, hundreds of men and women were trapped in planes and buildings, praying that God would rescue them so that they might live, but they died.

The scripture at the beginning of this chapter gave an account of the Babylonians, who lived northwest of the Persian Gulf. Sometime around 630 BC, they began to assert themselves against the Assyrian Empire, and they became the strongest world power at that time. But they were as wicked as the Assyrians.

- Verse 9—they loved to collect captives.
- Verse 10—they were proud of their warfare tactics.
- Verse 11—they trusted in their military strength.

They were a proud nation and bragged of their strategies, their large armies, and all their weapons of war that they would use to destroy their enemies.

But you are pure and cannot stand the sight of evil. Will you wink at their treachery? Should you be silent while the wicked swallow up people more righteous than they? (Habakkuk 1:13)

The Lord isn't really being slow about his promise, as some people think. No he is being patient for your sake. He does not want anyone to be destroyed, but wants everyone to repent. (2 Peter 3:9)

God is not slow. He is on his own timetable and will answer our prayers in the right time. We must hold fast to our faith and ask for his guidance and his will. He will always see us through our troubles.

16

If Only My Head Were a Pool of Water

If only my head were a pool of water and my eyes a fountain of tears. I would weep day and night for all my people who have been slaughtered.

—Jeremiah 9:1

Jeremiah was concerned about his people. They lied and were deceitful, and they practiced adultery and many other common sins. He was very angry at them for all the sins they committed, but he showed compassion to them because he cared for them and wanted them to turn back to God.

Look at what Jesus said when he stood before Jerusalem, the city that would neglect him:

"O Jerusalem, Jerusalem, the city that kills the prophets and stones God's messengers! How often I have wanted to gather your children together as a hen protects her chick beneath her wings, but you wouldn't let me" (Matthew 23:37).

Look at what Jeremiah said: "My grief is beyond healing; my heart is broken" (Jeremiah 8:18). He was pleading with God to save his people from the sinful things in which they had been involved.

Jesus said, "And now look, your house is abandoned and desolate" (Matthew 13:38). Jesus felt the hurt because soon the city would be destroyed.

People tend to admire three things about others: wisdom, power, and riches. God puts a higher priority on knowing him personally, and he wants us to live lives of righteousness and love.

"And if you still refuse to listen, I will weep alone because of your pride. My eyes will overflow with tears, because the Lord's flock will be lead away into exile" (Jeremiah 13:17).

The Jewish leaders had refused God's offer for salvation in Jesus Christ when God himself visited them, and soon their nation was destroyed. The people suffered greatly because of their sins. God would not turn away from the Jewish people who disobeyed him, but he would visit them again. Just as God did not turn away from the Jewish people, he will not turn away from us when we sin. He will offer forgiveness when we repent from our sins and follow after him.

When we accept him in our lives, he gives us eternal life.

17

Quack Doctors

I always have been fascinated with an old saying I've heard on many occasions and that I've read in the Bible.

The mention of quack doctors is written in Job 13:4—"As for you, you smear me with lies. As physicians you are worthless quacks."

Webster's New Collegiate Dictionary defines quack as "a pretender to medical skill and pretending to cure diseases."

> I am against these false prophets. Their imaginary dreams or flagrant lies that lead my people to sin. I did not send or appoint them, and they were no message at all for my people. I the Lord have spoken. (Jeremiah 23:32)

In Jeremiah's time, those who claimed to speak for God were often guilty of representing a deity they thought of as limited and localized—a neighborhood god. Their gods frequently had limited interests and shortsighted awareness.

We must accurately communicate and live out God's Word. As you share God's Word with friends and neighbors, they will look for its effectiveness in your life. If it hasn't changed you, why should they let it change them?

If you say it, make sure you live it.

18

Windbags

God's prophets are all windbags
who don't really speak for him. Let
their predictions of disaster fall on
themselves!

—Jeremiah 5:13

Windbags were referred to as false prophets.

Therefore, this is what the Lord says:
I will punish these lying prophets,
for they have never spoken my name
even though I never sent them.
(Jeremiah 14:14)

Jeremiah was reminding Judah of the sins they
had committed. Jerusalem was the capital city and

center of worship for Judah. God was willing to spare the city if they could find only one person who was just and honest.

He made a similar statement in Genesis when speaking about Sodom and Gomorrah:

> Finally, Abraham said, "Lord please don't be angry with me if I speak one more time. Suppose only ten are found there." And the Lord replied. "Then I will not destroy it for the sake of the ten!" (Genesis 18:32)

You may represent the only witness for God to many people.

> Goodness makes a nation great, but sin is a disgrace to any people. (Proverbs 14:34)

Think how significant your testimony may be in your community.

> You are the salt of the earth. But what good is salt if it has lost its flavor? Can you make salty again? It will be thrown out and trampled underfoot as worthless. (Matthew 5:13)

Nothing but honesty is acceptable to God.

> Lord, you are searching for honesty. You struck your people, but they paid no attention. You crushed them, but they refused to be corrected. They are determined with faces set like stone; they have refused to repent. (Jeremiah 5:3)

> Yet even in those days I will not blot you out completely, says the Lord. (Jeremiah 5:18)

The Lord comforted Jeremiah with the knowledge that the destruction would not be total, and he prepared the prophet to respond to those who wondered why the Lord would bring such severe judgment upon them.

Lesson for today:

1. Be completely honest.
2. Be willing to change.
3. Be willing to lay out your life before God, that God may enter and begin rearranging your life.
4. Allow God to work change in you because as you hear the story with ears opened by the

Holy Spirit, you will hear it as you haven't heard it before.

God's message will never change you unless you heed it.

Don't listen to windbags.

19

Silent Watchdogs

For the leaders of my people—the Lord's watchmen, his shepherds—are blind and ignorant. They are like silent watchdogs that give no warning when danger comes. (Isaiah 56:10)

Blind guides! You strain your water so you won't accidentally swallow a gnat, but you swallow a camel! (Matthew 23:24).

The watchman's business was to look after the souls of men and feed them with knowledge and understanding. But they were not qualified to accomplish that; they were blind and ignorant of the knowledge of things divine and spiritual. They did not know the meaning of scriptures or the way of salvation by Christ. The Spirit of God had not come into their hearts, so they were spiritually unfit to be watchmen.

A watchdog is not of much benefit if it will not bark at the noise of a thief or when it's approached by another fierce animal. If the shepherd's dog will not warn him of a wolf, what good is the dog to him?

Christian television and radio are filled with teachers who claim to be living in God's lavishness. They teach others that wealth and health is the measurement of maturity.

> Some people may contradict our teaching, but these are the wholesome teachings of the Lord Jesus Christ. These teachings promote a godly life. Anyone who teaches something different is arrogant and lacks understanding. Such a person has an unhealthy desire to quibble over the meaning of words. This stirs up arguments ending in jealousy, division, slander, and evil suspicions. These people always cause trouble. Their minds are corrupt, and they

have turned their backs on the truth.
To them, a show of godliness is just
a way to become wealthy. (1 Timothy
6:3–6)

We should watch our lives and live according to the Word of God. Then we can live a wholesome, respected life, and people will see Christ in our lives as we live it day by day.

Keep a close watch on your heart.

20

Soul Therapy

This is what the Lord says; "Stop at
the crossroads and look around. Ask
for the old, godly way, and walk in
it. Travel its path, and you will find
rest for your souls. But you reply, No,
that's not the road we want!"

—Jeremiah 6:16

In most cases we know the right way to go, but we
sometimes go the wrong way and do the wrong
things. This causes us great heartache, and we
find ourselves on the wrong road, which leads to
destruction.

Our souls need therapy every once in a while to
get us back on track to follow God's will in our lives.

> Then Jesus said, "come to me, all of
> you who are weary and carry heavy
> burdens and I will give you rest. Take
> my yoke upon you. Let me teach you,
> because I am humble and gentle at
> heart, and you will find rest for your
> souls." (Matthew 11:28–29)

There are many therapists in our society today. They offer therapy sessions for just about everything in the world to help us through life's difficulties, which come almost on a daily basis. People spend many dollars over many years, trying to get help for various reasons.

However, the greatest therapist is Jesus Christ. He will take away all of our problems, disappointments, and financial and health concerns if only we will put our trust in him.

Our souls need therapy.

21

Following the Wrong Crowd.

You must not follow the crowd in doing wrong. When you are called to testify in a dispute, do not be swayed by the crowd to twist justice.

—Exodus 23:2

The above verse plainly instructs us not to follow the wrong crowd. The pressures of parents, siblings, friends, coworkers, TV commercials, and other things seem to distract us from doing what is right. Christ set the example when he was here on earth and gave us grace in accepting us into his kingdom.

Too many individuals, young or old, are caught up in the everyday expression, "Everyone is doing it, so why can't I?" Sometimes doing the right thing is not the popular thing and may cause us to lose some friends along the way, but being honest is the right thing in the long run.

The crowd is often wrong! Let me give you some examples of this statement:

1. In the days of Noah, the crowd perished and only eight survived (Genesis 7:13).
2. After the flood the crowd wanted to build a city and a tower, and they did not want to fill the whole earth, even though God told them to do this (Genesis 11:1–9; compare to Genesis 9:1–7).
3. In the days of Abraham, the crowd wanted to worship idols, including Abraham's family (Joshua 24:2).
4. In the days of Moses, the crowd worshipped the golden calf (Exodus 32).
5. In the days of Joshua and Caleb, the majority of the spies were afraid to conquer the land. The majority did not believe God (Numbers 13 and 14).
6. Jesus said that the majority (the crowd) was headed for hell, and the minority was headed for heaven (Matthew 7:13–14).

7. It was the crowd that yelled, "Crucify him!"
    (Matthew 27:22–23).

See how Pilate followed the crowd in Mark
145:15.

> So to pacify the crowd, Pilate released
> Barabbas to them. He ordered Jesus
> flogged with a lead-tipped whip,
> then turned him over to the Roman
> soldiers to be crucified.

There is a cost in following the Lord.

> Don't begin until you count the cost.
> For who would begin construction of
> a building without first calculating
> the cost to see if there is enough
> money to finish it. (Luke 14:28)

If you were to take a strong stand for the Lord,
what would be the cost? What might happen to
you? Look at the minister who was put in jail in
Iran for his faith. Was there a cost for him? Yes,
there was.

What would you say about the person who has
one foot on the Word, and one foot in the world?
This is the person who is riding the fence, who tries
to follow Christ and also the crowd.

I want to challenge you. The next time you see two people who are walking in opposite directions, try to follow them both.

22

Tasteless White of an Egg

Don't people complain about unsalted food? Does anyone want the tasteless white of an egg?

—Job 6:6

Many restaurants have egg-white omelets on their menus now because such omelets have fewer calories and are high in protein. Many diets list egg whites as good for you because they also are low in cholesterol.

If you are on a diet, you should eat only the egg whites, which will give you a high amount of protein with lower fat content. Does this make sense? It does to me because I've heard a lot about high-protein diets these days.

Job had something else to say about it: "My appetite disappears when I look at it; I gag at the thought of eating" (Job 6:7).

Job was in such discomfort, and he just wanted to die. God wanted him to trust him during this difficult time in Job's life. Our struggles may seem large or even small, but God wants us to trust him in everything because he cares for us.

> And we know that God causes everything to work together for good of those who love God and are called according to his purpose for them. (Romans 8:28)

We must realize that God works in every situation. Sometimes when adversity comes our way, we ask, "Why me, God?" Having trust in God is a wonderful thing because he cares for us and desires that we walk with him through all things that come our way.

> Furthermore, because we are united with Christ, we have received an inheritance from God, for he chose us in advance, and he makes everything work out according to his plan. (Ephesians 1:11)

Christ died on the cross just for you and me and said he would never forsake us or leave us. He is right beside us, each and every day.

Job said that Eliphaz's advice was like eating the tasteless white of an egg. When people are going through severe trials, ill-advised counsel is distasteful. They may listen politely, but inside they are upset. Be slow to give advice to those who are hurting. They often need compassion more than they need advice.

We sometimes think that life should be fair. But what if it's not? What if the scales are already tipped? Do we ever examine the justice of this? Most of us do not question those things that are considered "normal"—those things with which we were born. We have no control over them. It is the hand we were dealt at birth.

Job had a right relationship with God. He was not guilty of the sins of which his friends accused him.

Job was a righteous man.

23

Extras

In my research and studies, I found many things that I want to share with you. I haven't commented on these, but they will give you additional scriptures you can explore for yourself.

These are listed by topic, along with the Bible references where you can find them.

Smell of the outdoors—Genesis 27:27

Generic name for both sexes—Genesis 5:2

The first person to be embalmed—Genesis 50:26

Wrestling with God—Genesis 32:24

Tar used instead of mortar—Genesis 11:3

Fast food—Genesis 18:6–8

Did God ever change is mind?—Exodus 32:14

Just stay calm—Exodus 14:14

Community of troublemakers—Exodus 16:2

An ox knows its owner—Isaiah 1:3

Twisted chariot wheels—Exodus 14:25

Whining—Numbers 11:10

Standing between the dead and the living—Numbers 16:48

Grabbing the testicles of the other man—Deuteronomy 25:11–12

The fruit will drop before it ripens—Deuteronomy 28:40

Lap like a dog—Judges 7:5

The trees decided to choose a king—Judges 9:8

Right-handed murder—Judges 5:26

Finger thicker than my father's waist—1 Kings 12:10

Consulting old men—1 Kings 12:6

Mocking and making fun of him—2 Kings 2:23–24

I made a covenant with my eyes—Job 30:1

Disgusted with life—Job 10:1

Age of God—Job 36:26

Weathering the storms of life—Job 1:1–3

Maggots will find them sweet to eat—Job 24:20

Heart led by eyes—Job 31:7

A blast of his anger—Job 4:9

Hawk flies south—Job 39:26

Reduced to skin and bones—Job 19:20

The Lord answered from the whirlwind—Job 38:1

Storehouses of snow and hail—Job 38:22

Water jars of heaven—Job 38:37
I will cover my mouth with my hand—Job 40:4
My breath is repulsive to my wife—Job 19:17
Loss of speech—Ezekiel 3:26
Royal cosmetic—Esther 2:12
Pretended to be insane—1 Samuel 21:13
Foot soldiers hiring—2 Samuel 10:6
Conducting a census—2 Samuel 24:1
Hunting in snowfall—2 Samuel 23:20
Wear truth like an undergarment—Isaiah 11:5
You have become a worthless slag—Isaiah 1:22
Short beds—Isaiah 28:20
Plumb line measurement of righteousness—Isaiah 28:17
Everlasting name—Isaiah 56:5
Sun's shadow reversed—Isaiah 38:8
Lion eating straw—Isaiah 11:7
A drop in a bucket—Isaiah 40:15
Present your case—Isaiah 41:21
Testers of metals—Jeremiah 6:27
Bones spread out on ground like manure—Jeremiah 8:2
Thrown into a cistern—Jeremiah 38:6
Traps set to catch people—Jeremiah 5:26
Travelers shack—Jeremiah 9:2
Fair punishment—Nehemiah 9:33
Water gate—Nehemiah 8:1
A crooked bow—Hosea 7:16

Collapse in their mother's arms—Lamentations 2:12

Daily mediation—Joshua 1:8

Stones have ears—Joshua 34:27

People and animals wear garment of mourning—Jonah 3:7–8

Lazybones—Proverbs 6:6

Listen to my teachers—Proverbs 5:13

Don't get side tracked—Proverbs 4:27

Tie them on your fingers as a reminder—Proverbs 7:3

Don't waste your strength on women—Proverbs 31:3

The leech has two suckers that cry out, "more, more"—Proverbs 30:15

Work brings prophet—Proverbs 26:14

Fire goes out without wood—Proverbs 26:20

Useless as a paralyzed leg—Proverbs 26:7

Swallow your pride—Proverbs 6:3

Speaks without thinking—Proverbs 29:20

Dog returns to its vomit—Proverbs 26:11

Lying lips—Proverbs 12:22

Lazy people want much—Proverbs 13:4

Opinionated fool—Proverbs 18:2

Playing with fire—Proverbs 6:26–29

Be stingy and lose everything—Proverbs 11:24

Speaking without thinking—Proverbs 29:20

Keep your mouth shut—Proverbs 21:23

A lazy person turns over in bed—Proverbs 26:14
Make tempers flare—Proverbs 15:1
Belches out foolishness—Proverbs 15:2
Don't get sidetracked—Proverbs 4:27
A gold ring in a pig's snout—Proverbs 11:22
Trying to hold something with greased hands—
Proverbs 27:16
Flattering lips—Psalm 3:12
Worthless as a puff of wind—Psalm 62:9
Skip like a calf—Psalm 29:6
The Red Sea saw you—Psalm 77:16
Voice transmitted worldwide—Psalm 19:4
Talk is cheap—Ecclesiastes 5:7
Hard times—Ecclesiastes 7:14
Men who fear height—Ecclesiastes 12:5
If your boss is angry at you, what should you do?—Ecclesiastes 10:4
Let your words be few—Ecclesiastes 5:2
Like a fish in a net—Ecclesiastes 9:12
You can identify fools just by the way they walk down the street—Ecclesiastes 10:3
Hair was long as eagles' feathers—Daniel 4:33
Take a bath and put on perfume—Ruth 3:3
Wine drugged with myrrh—Mark 15:23
No need for expense money—Mark 6:7–9
The evil spirits begged him—Mark 5:12
This woman is wearing me out—Luke 18–5
A place where robbers hide—Luke 19:4

Produce fruit—John 15:16

Spilling out all his intestines—Acts 1:18

Helplessly conferred—Ephesians 4:17

The oil of joy—Hebrews 2:9

Learning by experience—Hebrews 5:8

Troubles prepare us to help others—2 Corinthians 13:4

Keep a clear mind—2 Timothy 4:5

Meddling in other people's business—2 Thessalonians 3:11

Snatching them from the flames of judgment—Jude 1:23

Angels securely chained in prison—Jude 1:6

People will be seeking death—Revelation 9:6

Beheaded for their testimony—Revelation 20:4

Printed in the United States
By Bookmasters